THE GOLDEN COIN

THE GOLDEN COIN

ALAN FELDMAN

THE UNIVERSITY OF WISCONSIN PRESS

The University of Wisconsin Press
1930 Monroe Street, 3rd Floor
Madison, Wisconsin 53711-2059
uwpress.wisc.edu

3 Henrietta Street, Covent Garden
London WC2E 8LU, United Kingdom
eurospanbookstore.com

Printed in the United States of America

This book may be available in a digital edition.

Library of Congress Cataloging-in-Publication Data
Names: Feldman, Alan, 1945– author.
Title: The golden coin / Alan Feldman.
Other titles: Wisconsin poetry series.
Description: Madison, Wisconsin : The University of Wisconsin
        Press, [2018] | Series: Wisconsin poetry series | Includes
        bibliographical references.
Identifiers: LCCN 2017042901 | ISBN 9780299316747
        (pbk. : alk. paper)
Subjects: | LCGFT: Poetry.
Classification: LCC PS3556.E458 G65 2018 | DDC 811/.54—dc23
LC record available at https://lccn.loc.gov/2017042901

FOR

REBECCA,

BRIAN,

AND **DANIEL,**

OUR GOOD FORTUNE.

CONTENTS

Acknowledgments   ix

I. FIRST LIGHT

Breakfast   3
The Far Away House   4
The March of Dimes   6
In the Cabana   8
What I Loved: Waiting for Our Luggage in Havana   9
Molly's Charm   11
The Art of Daydreaming   13
Bus Trip   15
Provincetown Harbor: *Last Chronicle*   16
A Journey   17
The Golden Coin   19

II. ROCKET'S RED GLARE

Scituate: September 2001   23
Putting Iron   25
A Language of One   27
On the Beach in Cassis   29
Idioms   31
The Poem I Lost Called "Cuba"   33
The Last Responders   36
Snagged   38
What He Remembers About His Trial   39
Alan in Poland   41
At the Meeting   43

III. HOUSE LIGHTS

Elegy for a House	47
Togetherness	49
No-see-ums	51
Alan, the Wheels on My Car Just Collapsed	53
Pencil	55
Future Value	57
If I Could Buy Anything	59
Akane	60
Squall	62
The Bell	63
What to Tell Martha	64

IV. FIRELIGHT

As I Was Carrying the Child	67
Herman Grad	69
Repairing the Deck	71
My Grandfather Speaks	73
Crossing the Durance	74
Life Is a Cruise	76
Waterfront Property	78
Fiddler Crabs	79
Alan in France	81
Desperate	83
A Voyage	85
Notes	87

ACKNOWLEDGMENTS

I am grateful to the publications where these poems first appeared:

Adirondack Review: "Idioms"
Antigonish Review: "Life Is a Cruise"
Ascent (online): "Crossing the Durance"
Catamaran: "A Voyage" and "Waterfront Property"
Cimarron Review: "What He Remembers About His Trial"
Cincinnati Review: "In the Cabana"
Cordite (online): "Future Value"
Dime Show Review: "A Language of One" and "What to Tell Martha"
Harvard Review: "Alan in Poland" and "Alan in France"
Ibbotson Review: "At the Meeting"
Mad River Review: "Breakfast" and "Putting Iron"
Miramar: "The Art of Daydreaming"
Poetry East: "The March of Dimes" and "No-see-ums"
Salamander: "Molly's Charm," "Scituate: September 2001," and "Fiddler Crabs"
Smartish Pace: "A Journey"
Southern Review: "As I Was Carrying the Child" and "Desperate" (under the title of "Daughter's Daughter")
upstreet: "The Last Responders"
Valparaiso Poetry Review (online): "Repairing the Deck"

"As I Was Carrying the Child" was also featured on *Poetry Daily* (poems.com) on November 17, 2015; "Fiddler Crabs" was featured on January 17, 2017.

Thanks to Carl Dennis, Jeffrey Harrison, and J. D. Scrimgeour who have been my first readers.

I

FIRST
LIGHT

BREAKFAST

This room comes with breakfast included.
It's the standard breakfast. The one you eat
each morning without care, the way your
eyes open, and you find out where you are,
whatever your dreams have been telling you.
If there are birds chirping, great, or if there are
bulldozers moving in on the construction site
next door . . . it's better to eat, to fortify yourself.

Everything can wait till after breakfast.
Have you had yours? The way our hands
carry water to the saucepan, the way
we blindly seek out the coffee, the egg
to rest in its shallow bath of water,
the way we spill little zeros into a bowl
and flood them with the primordial milk
of the first breakfast after the long fast of gestation,
the way the oranges give up their pulp and the melons
split open like the sun—all the days have
as their birthright such beginnings, such hope,
such lists of tasks to attempt. The day comes
with breakfast. Breakfast is included, yes.

THE FAR AWAY HOUSE

We must have thought we looked
responsible, freezing
in front of the green porch
of the ramshackle house
with the ominously sagging roof
we'd bought in our foolishness,
my beard just beginning to whiten,
your corkscrew ringlets still
gold-brown. We looked so proud
and oblivious, like new settlers.

We'd hired an honest carpenter.
It was almost winter
and the wind off the bay
was severe, inhospitable,
and made summer seem
theoretical. Did we look ahead
through the frozen rooms
to the kitchen we didn't yet have
to see this photo of ourselves
still on the refrigerator
among unimaginable grandchildren?—
it's their house now too, the one
they call the "the far away house."

To the parents that we were,
in the photo the carpenter took,
stuck now to the refrigerator
by a magnet shaped like a fish
and another like a daisy:
hats off to your faith.
That June we painted
every surface, our clothes
so spattered we threw them away,

and made a place destined
for our family forever—
that is, if you think of a house
as a state of feeling, the lilt
of wind off the ocean
through the gauzy curtains
before the grownups are awake.

THE MARCH OF DIMES

As a child I liked staring
at the miniature iron lungs
they placed on store counters,
just at eye level, and was impressed
to see coins of all kinds
tumbled together inside,
brown and silver,
like the mixing of the races.
And I respected the children
in real ones, who had their own
small bathyspheres,
and looked well-combed,
surveying their world through angled mirrors,
hoping to see their parents coming
through the hospital doors laden with toys!
But how could they play?
They could stare at toys, I supposed,
which is often fun, pretending
they were floating among them,
a phantasmagoria of fish,
the way I often stared at coins,
favoring dimes most, small and silver,
thinner than nickels and more valuable—
dimes that could cure polio
with their pure silver hearts,
with the profile of the late President
who cared for the least of us so much
he had the disease himself.

—

I understood how "The March of Dimes"
suggested the unconquerable military might
of kindness. But mostly I enjoyed
the thought of all those dimes
falling endlessly, like silver drops of rain,
till the hardened crust of the disease
was washed away.

IN THE CABANA

It was hard to stay sensible inside
the cabana, where he convinced a girl
to take off her bathing suit. Yes
it was simple lust, but epochal,
since he was young, like an epileptic
touched by the hand of a god
with about a thousand volts. She
was numinous, like a nude, and
nonverbally inspiring. The ocean
beyond the acres of sand was flat,
if seething. The sun itself
was inside the cabana, which smelled
of canvas sneakers and warm cedar.
Wasn't it the cabana he'd dressed in
a million times as a child, his suit
puddling on the floor and dripping
through the cracks to crater
the sand like a lunar mystery? But
suddenly it contained a lighthouse
confined to a space as tiny as a closet.
Every life should have this sunrise.
Does it matter who she was? It used to.
Now he thinks they'd simply become inhabited
by gods. Well, he was. He can't be sure
she felt anything but naked and appreciated,
having such influence on him, like a high fever,
or the shock of something scalding
served at a feast for the young
who've come down to live in adult bodies.
Afterward, they knew to exit the cabana separately,
as if they'd been taking turns in there, changing.

—

WHAT I LOVED: WAITING FOR OUR LUGGAGE IN HAVANA

The sense of full employment. Young people,
more than a dozen, standing around
in uniform, with epaulettes, the girls'
skirts worn very short, with lacy black
stockings, as if ready to go dancing
as soon as work ends. All with jobs
but not very hard ones, standing around
sometimes in conversation with each other
and the glamorous supervisor, her hair well-coifed,
also relaxed and chatting. Nobody
getting fired. And piles of packages
sent from America by devoted relatives
of the Cuban people, cocooned in plastic,
like giant eggs that will hatch into toasters
or microwaves or quilts or clothes for children.
And the passengers in our group being patient
about the Communist inefficiency
when the luggage doesn't arrive for us,
as though behind the rubber strips of the curtain,
where the luggage is supposed to come from,
men and women of Cuba are trying on our stuff
to see if anything will fit. And the whole
air of universal egalitarian frustration
(even the luggage of the natives doesn't come).
And our group of tired passengers
trying to be chipper, trying to learn what we can

about the country, while never getting any luggage,
never being allowed out of the terminal
into the waning light of the countryside,
into the cloudy, normal, embargoed light,
and the guide suffering from impatience too
with the snaggle of bureaucracy in his homeland.
And one of the guards with a little spaniel
who might be expected to sniff for explosives
in some other country, but here
just sniffs randomly, like any dog,
and lies down on the cool cement floor
with all four paws stretched out,
enjoying an unusually easy and pleasant life,
free from hunger and want, easeful and secure,
since some dogs are luckier than others, even here.

MOLLY'S CHARM

"So much charm, and such a fierce flame,"
I woke up thinking I'd write on her card
after I heard at work that she'd chosen
hospice instead of further treatment.

"No flowers," she'd commanded. So I imagined
her in a flowerless room at St. Patrick's Manor
surrounded by nuns, yet directing the way
she chose to die, at least a while longer.

She always reveled in a "leadership role"—
a political genius, who could no more refrain
from brilliant attacks to sink a perceived rival
than Mozart could have stopped inventing melodies,

all while pretending to praise and defend him—
like the time she "defended" me by saying,
at a meeting of hundreds, that I was right
to fire a man because he hated women,

which led to him suing me in federal court
for bias, while she seemed genuinely terrified
he was after her. How *could* I trust her?
Her brightness? Her easy assumption

we were both on the same good side
of everything, and against mere selfishness?
All the stuff I'll be sure to mention
when my turn comes to offer her eulogy . . .

But I can remember decades ago
when she seemed a romantic figure at the office,
her kids young, her husband prosperous, and she
was campaigning for McGovern. And she'd sail

past my door, or stop and beam at me
as if it was a special pleasure to see me—
a special pleasure to see any of us really—
her charm bathing me in good feeling

the way a woman's beauty can, like radiation,
even if you hardly know her. And yet part of it
was the way she always managed to be young,
as though momentous things were just now

happening to us, and the world was new.

THE ART OF DAYDREAMING

If she asks what you're doing,
say you're resting.

If she comes into your room,
close your eyes, since your eyes
are quite useless anyway:
the lake you're imagining
glimmering through the pine trees
is far more distinct
than the actual bureau with her jewelry box,
the laundry hamper, and the neighbor's gray roof
streaked with snow.

If she asks are you feeling OK,
say yes, you're fine.

It's not that you don't love your life at this moment,
but you love some of the earlier chapters too—
the lake house, with its crowded attic
and the cedar closet, which you are revisiting
by inhaling the scent of little cedar balls—
(there was a large cedar closet in the attic)
that are said to be safer than mothballs
(whose smell evokes the winter before
when your grandmother was still alive).

In the lake house your bed had a satin coverlet.
An artist had applied silver leaf and painted flowers on
    the walls.
You listened for the whine of an outboard.
You were in love, hopelessly, with the girl across the cove.
This is all very much like Proust.
But this isn't involuntary memory.
This is quite hard work, in fact.

Try to walk past the boat house down the driveway
paved with blank white tombstones
(bought on sale from a quarry by your doctor uncle)
and recreate how bored you could be, and how happy.
Most of all, try to recapture how the future felt
back when you were all future:
designing tall towers of glass on a new planet
circling a double star.

BUS TRIP

When she leans her head against me, tired,
in the midnight bus coming from the airport,
the lights sweeping along the tinted windows,
her head not nearly reaching my shoulders,
I think I know what the Buddha means
by "the smile," the way the soul bursts open
appreciating a sensational joke.

I who liked to lean against my grandfather
because his shirts from the laundry smelled so fresh,
and because of his tolerance, his natural joy to be hugged
(some men don't like it, my father did not),
I am suddenly revealed to be the grandpa!—
magic!—a scarf has turned into a pigeon.

All week we've lived together in Mexico.
Some nights she ended up sneaking into bed
with my wife and me—and now, returning,
she chooses me to use as her pillow.

The bus feels cold. Not like last week—
old school buses that were like tin ovens
jouncing over potholed roads, the windshields
spiderwebbed with cracks. No, there
our relationship was more intellectual:
Why were Mexican kids sitting impassively?
Because they weren't used to getting things?

But now she's not demanding my opinion.
No more discussions. She only needs
something comfortable to smoosh
against, a soft wall beside her.

PROVINCETOWN HARBOR: *LAST CHRONICLE*

Each year I sail up here, and anchor,
to steep myself in loneliness, far from the other boats.
Of course I have my books. In *The Last Chronicle*
Mr. Harding is dying, a sweet man, much loved,
who only turns sweeter with age. Do you think
he enjoys being alone with his memories? No,
he wants to have people by him. Not only
Posy, the five-year-old, but his two
redoubtable sons-in-law and his daughters,
a little town of love. He wouldn't want
to be on a boat. He wouldn't want to be floating
far from the shore. He wouldn't want the bell
in the library steeple to be the only one sounding.
On his daily walk, he loved to hear the bells
of his cathedral. Will I sell my boat at last,
tired of the loneliness? Will this be my last
night out here? So many people
care for Mr. Harding, he has no idea.
He wants his little family by him,
his little town of love. Look at the town now,
sparkling as the night comes on. And listen
to the faint music coming from a restaurant.
How small the town is really, along the shore
like a strand of stars. The town across the water.
The sound of a crowd singing in the restaurant,

and then the sighing of the wind . . .

—

A JOURNEY

"Everything's very small in France,"
I think the gas station attendant said,
trying to be friendly while washing my windshield,
and maybe that started it: after that
I realized I felt crowded in.
Not that home has any long vistas,
but the narrow streets, the buildings leaning
toward each other for centuries—it was beginning
to make me feel violent. I needed
a journey, a break from all this,
no sound but the wind. So I fought the traffic
and drove out here to the wilderness
below Ste. Victoire, Cezanne's mountain,
which from this angle looks like a tooth
biting at the sky. And beyond it I can see
vast stretches of France, maybe to the coast,
and hear nothing but the soothing message of the wind,
"Home soon. Shhh now." And I do feel calmer.

It's not that I'm from the vast spaces of the West,
or that I'm out on the empty sea that often,
but everything today seemed like traffic and lines
and even my friend Sabine's grave
that her husband Christopher took me to visit
seemed crowded. A cross here. A plaque there.
Though the olive tree he planted was spreading wide
in just these few years. I cleared away the cloud
of pale-green thyme growing across her name,
and thought of the bright colors she liked to wear,
and how much we laughed when we were together.

I wonder if this is what the dead hear,
this soughing sound, all their eternal lives.
Though it's laced with birdsong, still they're homesick.
If I listen I can hear all who have stopped speaking
breathe and release in one long sigh.

THE GOLDEN COIN

ON A TRAIN FROM BUENOS AIRES TO TIGRE

The sun rises out of the broad river—
"We've each been given a golden coin!"
you think as the railroad car sways,
filling with a buttery light.

You look around at the young,
how they enjoy themselves!—
as if they've been given this very morning
a treasure for their dowry.

You see the old dozing in their seats.
They have no need to open their eyes,
they know their stations by heart.
Even now they are thinking of this sunrise,
one more than they ever thought they'd receive.
They are so grateful! A golden coin!

I will never rust (goes the song)
We are rolling on tracks of silver, beside the river of silver,
but I am golden, warm as a loaf of bread . . .

When the train leans, the passengers lean too,
and hold on to their straps, their poles.
The car's crammed full today, full of treasure!—
so many travelers on their way to the beach.

That's why they're laughing.
They know how valuable they are,
how irreplaceable, even if they're poor,

though no one can be poor
when each morning without fail
another coin, a golden coin
rises out of the broad river.

II

ROCKET'S
RED
GLARE

SCITUATE: SEPTEMBER 2001

I've got the portable radio tuned to the news,
and they're singing "Battle Hymn of the Republic,"
its clotted lyrics sounding as though each singer
in the choir made up different words

until they get to "Glory! Glory! Hallelujah!"
The nation in mourning, and angry: In this town
of vulnerable beach shacks mounted on stilts,
two dancing schools and three barber shops,
even the dress shop has a big flag in the window
and the saleslady is wearing a stars-and-stripes sweater.

I usually forget to mount my boat's flag,
but it's flying, even in this storminess. The sea
is enraged, and the people on land are grieving,
and I'm holed up on board, like a survivalist.
Even my port lights have misted over,

though I have my radio. Human interest stories:
"When did you last see your wife?" the reporter asks
a husband whose wife was trapped on one of the planes.
He wants us to imagine our frequent, ordinary partings.
"Take care," she says. "Love you," he answers.
Tiny, but not completely perfunctory blessings.

I fire up the cabin heater, and make some soup.
If I were at sea, and not on a mooring, I'd have
no option but to keep sailing, and, in a way,
that sea is history: once something happens
we have no option but to consider that it has.

But this isn't history yet, it's still just news
to be added to the sea's reservoir of grief.
I need to switch over to some jazz station,
and rub the portholes clear. So many white caps,
the sea's not likely to drop its diatribe,
this slatting of the halyards against the mast—
a beating that keeps its rapid, unceasing count.

But the sea rocks us slowly. The pianist
thinks things over, chord after chord.
Oh I know, moans the bass. And the drummer
sets his snares hissing like banked fires.

PUTTING IRON

FOR SAMUEL HASS (1911–2000), MY FATHER-IN-LAW

Would you have laughed, Sam,
at how your putting iron came to
wander from office to office
where I work? I'd find it
like a long-necked goose
with a hard, dense head,
hiding in the shadow of the Xerox,
or months later in the men's room,
or near the palatial vending machine
with its rainbow colors so easily
shattered by the putting iron's
single-minded sense of purpose.

Remember Carla? She became frightened
a new client she'd been counseling
might be armed. "Send in
the blue folder," we were taught to say.
But would security really come?
So I brought in your putting iron
to keep by my desk. The client
seemed innocent, if violent,
like a bear. "Take your coat?"
said I, trying to sound welcoming.
The client wasn't armed. He wore
a rumpled white shirt. Peace
in his heart? Peace and complaining,
while I prepared the golf stroke
that could shatter his forearm.

I never took the club home.
It wandered like a steel emissary
of wariness, lost in a world
of ringing telephones and houseplants,
ready for some battle. A gleaming
steel spine of disinterestedness,
it's been resting beside the mail cubbies
that sniffer dogs sniff for bombs.

Oh, Sam, I didn't make this world,
and I don't play golf. You—
a socialist-pacifist, who spoke to strangers
the same way you'd speak to customers
or your own kids—sometimes crossed
that ocean of grass under a temperate
blue heaven to practice, or maybe
play nine holes. You never hated
anyone, except war mongers,
and to everyone else you offered
your open hand.

A LANGUAGE OF ONE

It begins with an idiot stare of hostility.

A man who bumps into us
as we're walking hand in hand
down a side street in Marseilles.

Perhaps it only means
When the sidewalk's this narrow
walk single file, tourist couple.

My wife checks her purse
(still there)
but I keep replaying this encounter—
the absence of any *pardon!*

as though the point is the young man's invisibility
You'll notice me now—

Would my weight trump his age in a fight?—
and I think about the book I'm carrying on ocean racing
and how men, young and old, battle a typhoon,
and it isn't always the old ones who die of exposure.

Or is he more like the typhoon?

Maybe he was at that demonstration this morning—
those flags on the plaza by the ferry landing,
those angry syllables telling me nothing,
that war dance like something from *Buffalo Bill's Wild West*,
while the yachts tack back and forth across the harbor.

So many languages I don't know how to translate.
So many expressions that are untranslatable.

Is that what I'll tell our friends when we get back?
Or will I reassure them that people the world over
are really the same, their smiles
worth a thousand words?

ON THE BEACH IN CASSIS

Do I want to be naked? Hardly.
But do I mind staring at naked women?
Christopher thinks this one, basking
on her green beach towel, reading from her phone,
isn't too bad, and wants to talk to her.
But what's the etiquette? We go back
to our manuscripts, to Christopher's poem
about a chameleon he was trying to smuggle,
that jumped out of his pocket, inopportunely,
right in front of the customs inspector.
Literary men! Both of us in long pants,
cautiously wearing sun hats. Should he
approach his poem from the animal's perspective
in a kind of fable? Distracted by the woman
on her green towel, he wonders if she's watching us.
Christopher tells me about a woman he once met,
half Lebanese, half something else—
he was reduced to fibbing he was half Polish—
oh, his mouth insisted on still talking,
though he knew she was dating some creep
after divorcing some awful husband.
"Well, that's the way with beautiful women,"
I tell him. "She'll keep meeting dolts."
Christopher agrees. "A sensitive man
would be tongue-tied." He decides
his usual compliments won't apply
if she's naked before he even starts.
"Madame, your beauty banishes all but fools."
That's what he tries out as he approaches her.
And she replies, "Then you must be a fool."

So that's the end of our little story!
Qu'a vist Pares e non Cassís a ren vist.
"You haven't seen anything if you've seen Paris but not Cassis." A Provençal saying.

IDIOMS

My sister, who never pleased our mother,
is being asked why. Why couldn't she have behaved
more normally?
                    "That's what rattled you,"
my sister tells her—never having believed
her mother loved her with the aching love
all of us easily saw.
                    "Alone is a stone,"
my mother answers—a flair for old sayings.
But it comes out sounding condemnatory
and stony.
                    "All your father and I ever wanted . . ."
she continues, as if that too isn't designed
to pierce a daughter's heart.
                    My father,
who never wanted anything from us, since wanting
was my mother's job.
                    "That's just water
over the dam," my mother says
to prove she can be tolerant
now that she's dead.
                    "But Turkey.
Why did you choose to live among the Turks?"
And my sister spits back at her, "Honi soit
qui mal y pense." And they never agree
about the Turks.
                    "I guess you made your bed,"
my mother says. And my sister answers,
"No use crying over spilt milk," which carries
a sting too,

since my sister never drank milk.
All of my mother's nurturing
was the wrong flavor.
                    And up here
in a world I must believe in amongst the clouds—
I dream I've gotten them at least to breathe
together calmly. Just breathe.
                            And I convince my sister
to let her mother embrace her
in her awkward fearful way. And my mother
to accept
            that what has come out of her
is untranslatable.

THE POEM I LOST CALLED "CUBA"

I admit I left out decades of dark history
in the poem I lost riding on the bus
in Havana. But I also captured how,
after years of surveillance and torture,
things might seem better now. Better
in some ways than my American homeland
I'm flying back to, since the airline
keeps trying to sell me all the products
that power our capitalist economy,
carping and certain in their right to assault me
with violent movies in which things explode,
or useless objects to make me fashionable,
and I'm already missing ad-free Cuba
where the only billboards celebrate victory
for the revolution, or feature the logo
of bearded Che with his beret, or offer
other encouraging slogans to the poor
as they wait patiently by the highway
to hitchhike, since they have few busses,
and our gleaming bus (where I left my poem
about Cuba) they know is only for tourists
from the land of wealth and self-interest . . .

In the poem I lost that I called "Cuba"
I found a way to praise the towns that ask children
to go house to house to spray for mosquitoes
without worrying any neighbor will harm them
(just as hitchhikers don't seem to worry about violence)
though they are a violent people, as you can see
in their up-tempo dances, violently celebratory.

In my poem I caught how they ignite
when they spot a friend, the hugs and shouts.
And, as well, the lack of a certain harried tension
that we see so often in my northern homeland
where the poor worry about eviction or the cost
of having to pay a doctor. Not in Cuba,
my lost poem explained in such a rousing way,
echoing the clear brook that runs through
"Guantanamera," which I sang under my breath
so soulfully, already wishing to return.

I admit that in the poem I left on the bus,
the one I dared to call "Cuba," I wrote
three whole stanzas about fatuous notions
promulgated by bureaucratic decree,
including how the salt shakers never work
because the health ministry says you can't
put rice in them—their rice has rat droppings!—
which you'd think can't be lyrical, I realize,
but it was in my poem, my *canto*
for the head-scratching dysfunction that opens
so much space for fellowship and joy.

And then, on the scribbled pages
the driver must be puzzling over now,
I had such an evocative passage
about the rest area where the bus stopped
so we could all go to the sad "baños"
with missing toilet seats, with thin cameos
of soap guarded by the weathered, enduring
bathroom attendant collecting a few coins

to lift her above her assured subsistence
into a romance of a little extra food—
and a passage about how people were dancing,
because, of course, there was a band
(all the rest stops in Cuba have bands!)
and my feet exploded into salsa, while my head
proposed "fierce," "eccentric," "good-natured,"
"florid," "loud," "misguided," "visionary,"
for this place that isn't about rest at all,
but Energy-in-search-of-joy, which is the name
of the movement they've given the world,
though they don't know it yet—but I know

the poem I lost described it, the one
that managed to leave out so much strife,
the one I simply named for them.

THE LAST RESPONDERS

One day a bomb goes off at a festival
filled with daydreaming, dawdling spectators
coasting between pleasure and boredom,
and everyone has to respond
because the shock of the sound
shakes the brain inside the casing of the head.

Who ties the tourniquets, carries away the victims
to the medical tents, the ambulances, the hospitals?
These are the first responders
we always want to have near us,
like parents who pull us back from the curb
when we don't see a bus bearing down.

But who are the last?—
the dumbstruck, spinning in their confusion,
the ones with no language at all, in fact,
just the reverberation of the completely nonverbal force
that is so emphatic that, in a single syllable,
it can undo many worlds?

These are the ones who may act, or not,
but whose minds refuse to respond. For them
the fragments of the blast
reverse their trajectories toward the zero moment,
then keep exploding. Let's not call it "processing"
or even the response of not responding—

---

the way they refrain from uttering
so much as an onomatopoeic sound
because, for them, the term hasn't been invented yet
to name what happened.

SNAGGED

On the same day Robin Williams
improvised a way to hang himself
using his belt jammed into a closet door
I was trying to free the prop of my boat
from an old, barnacle-encrusted mooring
that snagged it, diving
repeatedly, thinking each time
one more twist should do it, the problem
as simple as undoing a button
from a tight button hole,
my enemy, the water
choppy and cold, the problem
swaying in front of me with no
horizon, while a voice
inside me warned, *Stop!*
Consider hypothermia!
though another encouraged me,
One more twist, and your boat's free!
And so it finally was
when, trembling in the cabin,
unable to warm myself,
my legs shaking like a creature in its last
seizure, I passed the mirror
and saw a death mask
cast in tallow, a brother
I'd failed to look after
to keep from drowning.

WHAT HE REMEMBERS ABOUT HIS TRIAL

Sued by the American Civil Liberties Union!—
his old compadres (he, who carried their membership card
for more than a quarter century)—on behalf
of a visiting lecturer he refused to rehire:

He remembers the big stakes,
as if he'd progressed all the way in a game show,
as in *Champagne for Caesar*, one last simple question
with a life-changing fortune to hang in the balance,
("tell us your social security number") and he keeps the
    money . . .
and the sumptuous walnut paneling of the courtroom
and the panoramic view of the harbor from the balcony
with its carefree boats that opened before him
during recesses just outside the padded courtroom door.

And the attention—the jury across the room
like a Norman Rockwell painting of a cross section of
    Americans
staring at him—and his words, written as part of his daily
    work,
but carefully, it seems now,
blown up on big placards as evidence,
and quotable (by the lawyers, anyway)
and sounding pretty good! . . .

And his wife in the gallery gasping at the injustice of it all,
and his lawyer praising him, and their lawyer
trying hard to discredit him,
and the plaintiff looking like the Unabomber, Ted Kaczynski,
with his aviator's sunglasses, and Ted's allies, his own long-time
    colleagues
carelessly fabricating memories to hurt him . . .

and, oh, the cold he catches, the five pounds he loses, the suit
    he fits into
comfortably now, buttoning the vest,
and the story of his trial to tell at dinner parties,
and the judge, who seemed so careless and impartial,
calling a halt to the whole thing, and not even making him
    present his case . . .

and never having to lie about anything he'd done
and being told that he'd acted with integrity
and had nothing he should feel compelled to apologize for,
like a lens maker whose lenses focus sharply,
or a violin maker, whose instrument's tone is pure . . .

And seeing the wheels of justice grind slowly, but unceasingly
toward his exoneration, and the warm relief of his friends,
and the coda he heard from a young lawyer cousin
who knew someone on the jury
who said that they'd been wondering
why anyone would bother "that nice man" . . . him!

ALAN IN POLAND

I'm probably not very Polish-looking
judging from the people I pass
though my grandmother's family came from Warsaw—
bankers, she claimed; toll takers on a bridge, according to
    my grandfather . . .
I hate loud music, but love the musicians playing flute on
    the street today.
Sometimes, if I haven't heard really good live music in a while,
I cry. But here in Poland it's sunny
and I'm not crying.
My parents would have been killed soon after their wedding
if they'd lived here.
My own country's so young, fewer layers.
Here there are many, the top layer being the trees, all this
    vegetation
like a metaphor for forgiveness.
Yes, I still love the Danzig of Günter Grass,
where the kids would dive into the abandoned minesweeper
and chew seagull droppings on the breakwater . . .
even though it turns out Grass was conscripted into the
    Waffen-SS.
The young, all over the streets, don't care much about that.
They have T-shirts in English that refer to the heart:
You Rock My Heart
You Can See Into My Heart . . .
I try to see into their hearts,
but even this bright summer light isn't bright enough.
Poland can be lovely on a warm July day,
my T-shirt would say.
Music tells us how we could develop if we stopped hating.

I wish I could finally finish *The Tin Drum.*
I wish I could play Vivaldi on the trumpet,
or even in a jazz band,
or even on the street in Gdansk,
my coat spread out to receive people's zlotys.
My country is way bigger than Poland, and more varied,
but for now I only want to look at July
on the Baltic, and the beaches
filled with bodies that are just visiting,
maybe on vacation, or taking an impromptu day off from work
to bring their kids to the soothing, if forgetful sea.

AT THE MEETING

A storm was brewing in the time-darkened lobby
of the artists' co-op. It felt like history.
The artists didn't trust their president.
They tried to ask Perry Mason–type questions,
as if she'd tear off a mask, and say, "I confess!"
But, of course, artists are not detectives.
"It started with you!" said a willowy gray-haired man.
"Before you, we had peace!" But the president
sitting in the shadows of the lobby said nothing.

And then from the top of the stairs a woman spoke
who'd been painting outside all day. "Excuse me.
I'm not sure this is relevant, but the sky today?
I was outside, painting in the ball park,
and I looked up, and it was broad and blue!"

Everyone was silent, perplexed. On what side
of the dispute could the sky be?
As if Szymborska had come back to earth
to say that the sky is a window without a frame
crushing clouds as easily as graves, the sky
above and below us, as we fall from abyss
to abyss. Now the artists sat quietly relieved
and ashamed—to have forgotten we are all living
above and beneath the sky!

Now no one wanted to stay any longer in the lobby
of dark mahogany, that seemed lit by gaslight,
not even to talk about their work.
They simply wanted to get back to it.
The willowy man said, "We should all learn from our mistakes."
And the president wanted to return to her studio—
on the top floor, with windows facing north,
where the sun doesn't reach, but there's plenty of sky—
so she apologized as well, and slipped away.

III

HOUSE
LIGHTS

ELEGY FOR A HOUSE

The house is still there
on Google Earth, squatting
on its street in full sunlight,
its value in the current market
estimated by Zillow, its owner
named on the tax rolls of the town,
information publicly available by law.
But gone is the peach tree that slanted over the back yard,
the white dog who terrified, the cat
who brought his wife (we were told)
to have kittens in the safety of the deep well
where the basement window admitted a shadowy light.

In this house there was a grandfather who wore garters
to hold up his long socks; a grandmother
with a corset and a pink rubber ball
to squeeze and strengthen her hand after a stroke;
an uncle with eyeglasses framed in gold;
an aunt who handed the maid a banana
and told her to take it to the bank and cash it;
a tub with the feet of a great lion;
and a farm depicted on the wallpaper
exactly like its neighbor farms. We checked
on rainy afternoons, detail by detail,
in the prison of vast amounts of time.

And the cold spirits that blew up and down the laundry chute
in clouds of despair? How we pitied
their insubstantiality. How we would listen for them,
the ones who used to wear the clothing in the cedar closet,
or carry the dusty suitcases across continents
that no one can visit anymore, even on camels.

TOGETHERNESS

In my dream we are together
in the same house though not
always together but reading or painting
or thinking over plans in different rooms,

while in her dream we are sometimes
always together and sometimes not together
at all, while she is lost in her studio
overlooking the turnpike and I am miles

to the west in our house that seems
particularly empty to me, a house
with too many rooms, though usually
I like there to be a few empty rooms

between us, and I like silence, but I don't
like the perfect silence of emptiness,
the nights when the only voice is mine
inside my head, or hers, vivid and excited

on the phone, those long calls, those visits,
that disembodied voice—and that is why
life is a negotiation between her preferences
and my own embarrassed confession

that I don't like solitude the way
I once enjoyed it, when the kids
were noisy and demanding and I wrote a novel
up there in my study, a boring novel

about a man who finally finds his soulmate,
though now that draft seems so complacent,
as though she's a household goddess
blessing the premises and not intruding

on his time . . . whereas in the novel I'd write now
she'd probably be quite happy alone
and he'd be alone and hoping she missed him,
though that would be cloying, wouldn't it,

yes it would, so instead I'll describe
a sweet discord that won't resolve,
like a musical suspension, where the note
everyone in the audience expects

seems to take forever to arrive.

NO-SEE-UMS

"They must have a purpose," she says, of the bugs
tiny enough to fly through screens. "You're
becoming religious," I tease her.

I'm wearing a hat to fend them off,
and a sweatshirt. They bite any skin
they find. "They're a sign," I tell her,

"we're not in Paradise." We shouldn't be fooled
by the sapphire-colored sky, the gloss on the pine needles,
the crisp flag crackling on its white-painted pole,

or the clouds of leaf-laden branches shading us
with their billows. Does she wonder if the purpose
of the individual tree is to be part of that lush leaf canopy?

Or if we're here to help our local theater troupe
in their efforts to go to Scotland? Their benefit tonight
includes some Celtic songs accompanied by bagpipes.

Well, even an instrument like that must serve a purpose:
Our neighbor pipes "Amazing Grace" at dusk
as though he's providing a little funeral for the sun—

the sun in which the no-see-ums are dancing
like dizzy molecules in the beam of the spotlight,
till they drop, their bodies scattered like flecks of soot

on the table top in front of us. Though tomorrow,
if it's not too windy, still more will be zigzagging,
like piloted dust motes, or like sensations on their way
to become thoughts, with their tiny wings.

ALAN, THE WHEELS ON MY CAR JUST COLLAPSED

WHY ALL THIS LAUGHTER, ASKS THE BUDDHA, AND THE WORLD IS ON FIRE. —DHAMMAPADA

"Alan, the wheels on my car just collapsed!"
And you don't sound like you, but shattered,
a bit hoarse, no lilt of musical cheerfulness,
but something like the legs of a chair being dragged
over a hard floor. You know nothing about cars.
Oh, where are you? You say a street name
but I know nothing about our town's spiderweb
of roads. I'm so slow. So slow.

But then I'm out in the cold rain and on fire
with emergency. Ah, your poor crippled van.
And a little conference of men in green-brown fatigues
who have stopped to help, as if there's an army
we never see till we're wrecked, or fall through ice.

A blue bolt of malignant lightning: that's how
I imagine the car that nearly sideswiped you,
drove you into the curb. But you are not hurt.
The car is hurt. Your buoyant heart is hurt.

Oh, this is the news, but not the news
that shatters the globe of the sky.
I'd choose to be dead before you, you know,
though I know that's completely selfish . . .
Meanwhile, I give you my car to take to the party—

a friend's birthday party you were going to—
and I confess I feel quite wonderful,
like such a useful first responder!—

walking home through the rain.
The rain that waters the cemetery,
and the little experimental buds
of forsythia that will soon burst out
with the same traffic-lane yellow
as my parka. Yellow
the color of laughter.

PENCIL

I'm always afraid
I won't find one—
an ordinary pencil
the color of a school bus
or a windowless bullet train
of mysterious provenance,
its nose black
like a dog's curious snout,
and in back
the bud of an eraser
for what needs to be unsaid.

To this day,
in a million schoolrooms
filled with gleaming tablets
of heatless onyx,
and the cold light
of tyrannical radiation,
they are there. Pencils!
Children love forgiveness,
and the way they can be freshened
by a little trip to the sharpener,
and the secret, private pleasure
of the scent of the shavings,
like a hiding place
under an old staircase.

With pens, they write silently,
but with pencils, they must rub
something on the snow
of the paper
with a conspiratorial
whisper, constructing
the small uneven buildings
of their letters
into orderly streets
others can visit.

Even stumpy
they still work,
little beams of marigold-colored
light—no one's possession—
passed like a gift
from hand to hand.

FUTURE VALUE

My finance teacher, with a voice like Gandhi's,
is trying to explain the concept of future value.

He says we'll like finance, because it's like time travel.
He says it's nothing like accounting, which is all about

tallying up the deficits of the past. Finance, he says,
is all about the future, and so all of its answers

(he cheerfully tells us) are wrong.
Thousands all over the world, we're listening

to his lecture, and trying to solve the problems
that cast most of us into an ideal future of singing

the song of future value. The magic mirror of finance.
The telephone booth that takes us far into the future

on the day the final payment is made—then back
to calculating the present value of all those payments

down the sluiceway of time. Calculating
as if the winds of hazard and contingency

can be measured out to many decimal places
for my fellow students, faces glowing

from their screens, gazing at the heaven
we've always dreamed of—a heaven of ideas

that create value, the best ones attracting
the capital that is always hungrily searching.

So says the tiny head of my professor
who pauses from his work on formulas to stare at us

backward through the camera—each of us out there,
whether in St. Petersburg or Singapore—to say

that he believes we learn best when we have to struggle;
and that some things are too valuable to measure;

and here he offers love as an example, as if
he's used to assuming his students are young;

and that the problems on the test will be harder
than anything he's explaining to us now.

IF I COULD BUY ANYTHING

If I could buy anything, I'd buy light
in these dark winter months, with their narrow days,
the sun low and dim, as if I'm sick
and seeing the sky through half-opened eyes.
I'd buy a few weeks in a place by the sea
far south, where the gleam of the water
makes me squint, and a breeze touches
my bare arms repeatedly, doting on me.
I wouldn't go alone, either. I'd bring
an artist with me, who'd draw in bright colors
scenes of summer in a sunny place.
And I'd write poems with words like "gleam"
and "sparkle" and even "glare," and nights
would be balmy, thousands dining in the open air
under lanterns. And I'd be out on the water
whenever I could be—the sea sparkling,
the glare of white sails, and the gleam
of the boat's wake—and the only storms
would be brief ones, as if the earth
had a soft spot in her heart for me,
hugging me to her—I, her beloved—
and my actual beloved would smile at me
when I returned, her oil sticks
fanned out in a kind of rainbow
on the marble table outside our room.

AKANE

For nearly two weeks, I watched you
face us from the front of the bus, talking,
talking, as if it was obligatory
not to let the crowded towns and paddies
and nondescript, endless suburbs pass
without some voice-over to populate
this illegible country with human stories,
even personal, like when you were engaged,
briefly, and moved south to Hiroshima
to be with your fiancée, and your parents
went into mourning. It was so far!

You had the face, the strong chin of a boy.
You joked about your parents being grateful
by now if you married anyone! Was I right
that you felt only an ember of regret?

What were you thinking: A bus load
of *gaijin* substitute parents?
We liked it when you showed us pictures
of your tiny twelve-tatami-mat apartment,
as snug as a mouse hole, with little clues
about what you cherished. Your posters
from some of your favorite manga novels.
Your boxy little tub where you must have bathed
in a kind of isolated trance, utterly silent
after spending the day talking your brains out,

---

and timing everything, and counting us,
so as not to lose even one illiterate
to wander the sidewalks holding out a paper
with the name of the hotel so someone
would summon a cab, as if we were children.

When you walked us along the road the troops took
in the time of the Shogunate, sheltered by trees
so high we *did* look like children, lost in a fairy tale,
you seemed to allow yourself some silence.
Perhaps the place spoke for itself. It said
that we are not the large, romantic theme
of some symphony, but a flute player or harpist
hidden in the orchestra of the world.
Yet we'll remember you anyway, Akane,
your collapsible car antenna with its replica
of Mount Fuji you made from felt hoisted aloft,
and you still at your post, a faithful samurai,
as you watched the last of us board our trains.

But now that you're free? Are you climbing
the 800 steps to the temple you led us to
because you liked the monk? "For most of them
it's just a job." Are you ringing the giant bell
and listening to its echo ricochet
between the mountains? Will that help your soul
grow smaller, more collective, and restrained?
Or are you guiding another group already?—
rolling that small black carry-on none of us
was allowed to help you lift, shiny as armor,
along the platform where the *shinkansen*
opens with a whoosh, then whisks you away.

SQUALL

The sea and the air turned white, and my sloop
was knocked down on its side. Scared?
My whole brain was emptied of fear—since fear
implies a self—and what was left
was mere astonishment. "This looks like
a disaster movie," I remember thinking,
with the water blown by the wind into smoke.
That's how I understood I wasn't there,
though my life was. Somewhere else
on the bay a man died when his prop
got tangled in a lobster trap.
A fatal rush of adrenaline.
It was as though the world we see routinely,
a blue ocean with a green coast,
turned out to be a decorous convention.
And this roaring horror of whiteness
was what it concealed.
Death was a quaint idea.
This was obliteration. How long did it last
in its full outrage?—I couldn't say.
Probably minutes. But the mask was off.
Love was a pretense. The soul blown away
in sheets of brine. Then
it passed and left the bay
an angry dark blue
with a steep chop
and tossed boats coping.

THE BELL

Sometimes when our grandchildren are playing
(we like to bring them over to our house
to get them away from their glowing screens)

I hear the pure sharp note of the dinner bell,
the one that rang in my own grandparents' house
at six, exactly, and brought us all to the table.

Since *we* don't have that custom, I know
it's just our kids playing with a knicknack
they especially like at "Nannie and Grandpa's"—

the bell with a handle shaped like a sunfish
and a brass body inscribed with blossoms
the ancient Chinese would probably recognize—

the bell I've asked them *not* to play with,
or at least put away when they're finished—
that bell I've begged them not to lose.

Yet when they ring it I feel so happy.
Ching, ching. A Pavlovian response!
I'm a child too: as though my mother

has put soup out on the table, steaming hot,
and my grandmother is setting down her book,
and my grandfather is unfolding his napkin,

and I'll see them when I open the dining room door.

WHAT TO TELL MARTHA

"Do me a favor," said Martha. "If your walk's
better than ours, don't tell us."
A steep uphill with more expansive postcard views
each time we stopped for breath. We could see
Vesuvius, not erupting, across the bay,
Martha and the others too small to make out
but easy to imagine, up there in ecstasy
on top of the cone of ash. Our day?
Harder to describe, downplayed or not.
Back yards full of lemon trees. The smell
of grapes, or, occasionally, a hog.
The flat silver shine without a horizon
of the Bay of Salerno from St. Agata
at the top. Tired legs. A lunch
at a trattoria. The kids
horsing around, their dad cooking,
their mom the waitress. Italy!
so loamy and ancient. The path down
not too exhausting. But what to tell Martha
when she gets back from Vesuvius?
She chose the big mountain, the peak experience.
Like hanging by yourself from the chair lift
on Capri, that Martha swore put her in touch
with the gods. Or like the rainbow she saw
(though we didn't) from the bow of the ferry.
Nothing life-changing in the route we took,
if such change matters, since Martha's returned,
and based on what she spotted up on the mountain,
steam escaping from deep inside the crater,
an eruption's due, and then the best route won't matter,
only finding each other inside those clouds.

IV

FIRELIGHT

AS I WAS CARRYING
THE CHILD

As I was carrying the child into the house
from the car in the driveway, through the frosty air
that ate through even the thickest coat,

the garage door lifted, recognizing its code, and the walls
of the basement smelled like a root cellar.
As I was carrying the child into the house,

her bare feet dangling (she had kicked off her boots),
I thought, as anyone would, how light she was,
though heavier than before; how someday she'd learn

to keep her boots on (when she's too big to be carried)
and to be more tactful—"You're strong," she told me, "for
    an old man";
and how, for her, the thought of an old man's death

is a mere fact, the way water spills from a tipped bucket,
just as it should, so nothing in her affection
is due to pity, but comes from the simple pleasure

of being carried, quite high, by a being large
and kind enough to do it, like a monumental horse,
breathing clouds of vapor, its legs way down, moving

like something that falls, just a little, but doesn't, because
it's charged with a strength that's muscular, and electrical,
not mechanical, but responsive, and has a voice . . .

As I was carrying the child into the house
from the car in the driveway, through the frosty air
that ate through even the thickest coat—time

rose up and swept through me like a breath.

HERMAN GRAD

He was the oldest human I knew.
As a kid I dated all landmarks
as "older than Uncle Herman" or not as old.

My first boat was Uncle Herman's green steel rowboat
that came with the country house he left us
and that my father was eager to sell
(it needed too much maintenance) though it had frontage
    on a lake.
From this my life out on the water?

Rowing ashore today, I was thinking of him,
talking to him, really, about my life.
He was something of an intellectual. Loved Emerson
and would be glad, I think, to know I taught "Self-Reliance"
    in my classes.
Like my uncle, I became a doctor—sort of—
a doctor of poetry—and this summer
I've been re-teaching myself to play the flute.
He played the violin, lovingly, though not that well.
Can the dead hear the notes we play for them?
And would he be happy to know how I lead my life
with the leisure to take time off
to spend a day on the water,
or listen to the mute gospel of the marshes or the sand bluffs?

He only knew me as a cheerful, loquacious child,
the one who'd taken his hand whenever we went on walks
to warn him about cracks in the sidewalk.
He paid for my schooling, I found out years later,
reaching into my life
the way a surgeon like him touches you once,
only briefly,
usually for the good.

REPAIRING THE DECK

I'm so much quicker and younger, thinks the mind
while the body tediously bends and kneels with a drill
to back the ten-year-old screws out of their holes,

half of them breaking off, thinned by rust to crumbly
pieces of yarn. *I could do this in my sleep*, thinks the mind,
which has already been leaping around, considering the options

while the body has only one option: turn the boards over
so in the next ten years they'll dry out on the other side
and curl the other way. *The boards are repenting*,

the mind considers. *Now's their chance to flip over
and bare their shadow sides to the snow and sun.*
Or, the mind thinks, *I am undoing what I once did*,

unscrewing my own screws. With all these boards removed
and the sleepers exposed, the deck looks the way it did
that spring I came down and built it with our carpenter

who suffered from light deprivation over the winter
and needed someone at the work site for company.
But when I built it then, I thought only of the future,

of someday taking the boards up, as the body is now doing.
I didn't think about the past, of being old enough to rebuild
the same things I built ten years before, and from here

the mind goes on to consider Dad, even Grandpa,
and what they were like at this age, and did they
release a breath like an old bellows each time

they bent down and stood up? (They did.) But the body
ignores that. One damn board. Then another.
It wants to finish. Then rest. A sequence

clear as breathing. The mind considers its reply
but drifts around the deck, thinking silence is good
for a while. How free it would be, if—

keeping to itself—it never had to speak.

MY GRANDFATHER SPEAKS

Don't think I've forgotten what you did for me
just after Grandma died, when you were ten
and I was the age you are now.
You told your parents I could sleep in your room,
hardly complaining, though bad dreams
sometimes woke you. Mine, I mean.
I still cry out when I have them,
startling the dead, though all of them know me.

You were my kid, more than your silent father's,
but any guilt you feel about that
is probably appropriate and makes you
better. Always doubt yourself
and believe in yourself. That's my message.

Too bad you have your father's relaxed attitude,
almost welcoming old age, as if it's peaceful.
Well, don't fool yourself.
It's an abyss, as I always knew. I was a boy
when a high-rise collapsed on my family's house.
Mother and father dead.
Two older sisters dead. Younger brother dead.
Grandmother dead. And an uncle . . .

And I walked away alone.
Don't think I didn't wail like a frightened infant.
Probably that's the terrifying sound
you heard in the night
when I was just the age you are now.
Compared to that, being dead is nothing.

CROSSING THE DURANCE

"'He plunged to his death creeping around the ledge
of the granite tower of an old suspension bridge
crossing the Durance,' would be an incongruous way
to end my biography," is what I think
before I'm actually on the ledge and stop thinking.

My body feels so naked before gravity that my panic
at the thought of panicking and actually falling
needs soothing by some mature voice. But I'm old!

"This is probably the last physically daring stupid thing
I may ever do," I think. And when I make it
onto the bridge its splintered wooden walkway sways a bit
and is burnt through in places. Yes, it looks like a ruin,
like a sun-scorched ancient wooden road that ends
with a high cinderblock wall (which is why
one has to climb around the tower), while below,
the Durance is dry. A few frog ponds. A shallow
sheet of water covering some blanched rocks.

This looks like the end of the line. Christopher
took Sabine here, before she died. I wonder
if something satisfied them about this enormous metaphor
for doom. Maybe the bridge will last long enough
for me to creep back around the edge of the tower and exit
while my friend says, "Bigger steps. Place your hand here.
Now here." Maybe some might consider it cathartic
to burn one's bridges, though the voices of my ancestors
supply a chorus of dismay. I'm finished, I realize,

---

though I don't fall. I've crossed and made it down,
and now what? Perhaps to take more pictures
so I'll remember how my thoughts fell away,
my whole being emptied out, as if I'd never been born,
and my astonishment to find myself back
with my body, to go on with my journey.

LIFE IS A CRUISE

"I wonder if the world is anchored anywhere,"
Melville asks, as if we're all voyagers
on his whale ship. But for most of us
there's no sudden shock of collision
with the broad inscrutable forehead of our fate.

No, our ship's pool sloshes gently. There's music
playing softly. And if we don't like it
we can plug in our earphones and listen
to a book that takes place on land. It starts
with the hero's birth, and brings him
to a state of happiness. Of course we've read it
before. And that's part of the pleasure—
the way it reawakens the memory of pleasure.

And the port we're headed for?—
don't think about that now.
Focus your eyes on the sea.
How some waves break,
but most don't. And so
little flecks of white appear
on the blue, nubbly surface.
There's no pattern at all
except there's never a pattern.
And at times having no pattern can be soothing.
There's a wave breaking nearby. There's one
midway. And at the sea's edge
a tiny fleck in the distance . . .

They resemble nothing at all.
Not the stars that wink randomly,
nor the piercing flares of light
off windows in the city near
to sunset. I've read the human mind
can't produce randomness,
but the sea can. And also
it's impossible to produce silence.
Yet the ship can almost do that:
the steady hush of its motion.

There's nothing wrong with celebrating
the steady progress along the sea road
that's not a road. Nor even a history
made up of choices. And if you think
one ship might be as good as another
(if you have that sort of temperament)
you'll enjoy an easy passage in fine weather,
enough to wonder, at least for a time,
if you're among the fortunate.

WATERFRONT PROPERTY

It's good to have read, so that you can find a name
for what you see. Gooseberries. Do you remember that story
by Chekhov? An owner of a humble estate
thinks it would be paradise to grow them. A glory
to show off the sour fruit to visitors. What
are we doing here? I ask myself. Growing gooseberries.
Just another way to live for things, but not
the soul. And yet the crowds that come by car, by ferry,
to stare at the sea, feel it makes them larger.
And the owners of these houses, jumbled against the ocean,
must believe they've come as far as they can, to the margin
that divides one's possessions from the inexpressible: Here is
    the protean
nothingness of sheer existence, the sea, and here
is my property. And me. And the gooseberries I hold so dear.

FIDDLER CRABS

They look too busy to retire.
Or else some government has cut their pensions
and they have no option but to remain industrious,
whatever it is that they do, exactly,
at certain hours, when the tide has fallen.

They scurry from hole to hole in great droves
of rush hour traffic, each carrying his single claw,
an outsized instrument of self-protection,
though I prefer to think it really *is* a fiddle,
and they are afraid of being late for rehearsal.

Just to see them makes me feel alienated and idle,
heading for my boat where I sit reading, or set sail alone—
so I tap them with my foot, just to be playful,
but can't really hurt them. They suffer
their brief setback in a stolid, manly way,
always finding a little foxhole for refuge.

They reassure me that way, a population
that lives for work and not for war,
disregarding my mock attacks from the air.
Like the Dutch, a small, industrious nation,
practical and modest, their domestic life
orderly, even sacred—or so I suppose,
though no tiny Vermeers record it.

I love the way they keep their private lives to themselves,
menacing an intruder with their outsized claw,
and accepting grief—their hollow carapaces
on the deck of my boat, all the meat eaten by gulls—
without posting about it, or staging ceremonies.

"We're beneath your notice," they might say,
"or so we hope. Free to worship as we choose."
And as for me, standing above them, alien,
and bemused by their diligent behavior,
aren't I the lost one? They're rooted securely
in their mud cities and their daily round—
and every one of them can play his part
in the concerts they offer at evening
to the setting sun.

ALAN IN FRANCE

I am not a young American chemical engineer living in Paris
(though Lesson One teaches me to say that).
I'm a retired American living in Aix-en-Provence
where all the little shops play American songs.
(America, my country, where they misconstrue liberty
to mean extra-low taxes for hedge fund managers.)

My wife makes vividly colored paintings, often of France,
of old stone villages with arches, with flowers.
And Camus' molecules are in the tassels of grass
I carry in my wallet—Camus who described the lives
of the silent poor. How can I not love France?

I like to go to concerts in old churches and cry.
That's me, with the white-gray beard, looking somewhat rabbinic.
My country seems to need to punish the poor.
I like to see hunger managed. Desperation managed.
And the heat of the world managed, the way here
the trees are sublimely managed along the roadside.

Let's say music is as close as we get to heaven.
Though I play French horn and blockflöte (neither well),
I'll never get to heaven, I fear. Only France.
France whose grapes weigh more than all the guns in my country,
if we count all those gnarled ancient vines still uttering leaves.
France that pays young women to have babies.
France that sends its dispirited unemployed to spas.

When I was a child it took seven whole days
to reach here in a ship twenty blocks long.
The war was just over. People were missing legs.
But where else could the joys of peace be better celebrated?

Sixty years later, today, on the Cours Mirabeau,
they think it's time to *couper* the giant plane trees
like so many asparagus in a garden.
And that fellow, in the bleached, abundant, shadeless sunlight,
in front of the monumental fountain
symbolizing rivers tamed, canalized, and pure—
that one is me. Or rather, me in France.

DESPERATE

She is arriving just as I'm leaving
I think in my sorrow as I catch her body
squirming like a taut fish as she swims
as far as she can on one enormous
heartfelt breath. Or we stare
eye to eye, her face covered in droplets,
as if our ship is sinking.

Oh, such a doomed romance! She
is incredibly rich, has so very many years,
while I'm running thin. Won't attend
her wedding, very likely, or know
what patients she'll treat with her brilliant
kindness. Oh, little firmly packed fish!

Back she swims toward her mother—
her mother substantial and wise and forbearing—
whom I once taught to swim this way,
enjoying the luxury of infinite repetition.
Back and forth. This one could go farther—
almost forever—if she'd condescend to learn
to breathe. But she's learning everything else
so readily. Like "desperate." I said it
in front of her once, and since then
it pops up in her speech, so naturally.

As if she's always known it. She's "desperate"
for dessert, or feeling "desperate" if her sister
beats her at cards. Her "desperate" so
immediate compared to mine, I think.

That is, until she scrabbles into my arms,
and I'm wildly desperate to hold her.

A VOYAGE

I can't even take my glass of grapefruit juice for granted,
    after reading about the voyage of the *Endurance*,
twenty-two men with nothing to eat but penguin meat, after
    they'd eaten their dogs,
their ship, by then, long gone, crushed to splinters by
    implacable ice,
their cozy home for a year reduced to trash buried by snow.

I'm locked in my chair, staring at their young faces. Of
    course, they're all dead
but from other causes—the Great War, or alcoholism (due
    to boredom?), or simple old age—
their leader determined not to lose one of them, even the
    ones he didn't like.
In fact, the worst ones he put in his own tent, lest the other
    men kill them.

Frozen to my chair, I stare at their faces in a hundred
    photos,
young men, all dead now. How they put aside their quarrels
and saved each other, though the world couldn't save itself.
They are sitting around the night watchman's stove, back
    when they still had a ship.

Sitting by the stove on a ship trapped in Antarctic ice, in
    their rough sweaters and watch-caps,
they are staring into the fire, as real as any of us,
that is, for as long as any of us can be real,
as if Rembrandt had arranged them, asymmetrical,
ready to pose, lit by one source of light.

NOTES

"Provincetown Harbor: *Last Chronicle*": Septimus Harding is a retired warden and precentor living at Barchester deanery in Anthony Trollope's final novel in the Barset series. He is the title character of the earlier novel, *The Warden*.

"On the Beach in Cassis": *Qu'a vist Pares e non Cassis a ren vist*—that is, "If you've seen Paris, but not Cassis, you haven't seen anything"—referred originally not to the cities themselves but to the versions of an eighteenth-century statue and fountain, the larger in Paris, the smaller (and finer one, according to many) in Cassis. While not quite the boast it seems, it still sounds like a challenge to look for unexpected, less celebrated wonders.

"Idioms": "Honi soit qui mal y pense" means "evil to him who evil thinks."

"Alan in Poland": My parents were married in July of 1939, two months before Germany invaded Poland. Of about 1,800,000 Polish Jews at the time of the invasion, only 380,000 were left alive in 1945. The Danzig (Gdansk) teenagers in Grass's *Cat and Mouse* like to chew dried seagull droppings.

"At the Meeting": Perry Mason is a criminal defense lawyer who is the main character in more than eighty novels and short stories by Erle Stanley Gardner (1889–1970). Mason usually proves his client's innocence by forcing another character to confess. Polish poet Wisława Szymborska (1923–2012) was awarded the Nobel Prize for Literature in 1996.

"Alan in France": "Misconstrue liberty" because the biblical meaning—as in the Liberty Bell's inscription, "proclaim liberty throughout all the land" (Leviticus 25:10)—carries the connotation of responsibility for others. In fact, the biblical Hebrew is *dror.* For example, Jeremiah 34:17, "to proclaim freedom [*dror*], each man to his brother." I'm indebted to Professor Bernard Horn for this insight.

WISCONSIN POETRY SERIES

Ronald Wallace, *Series Editor*

New Jersey (B) • Betsy Andrews

Salt (B) • Renée Ashley

Horizon Note (B) • Robin Behn

About Crows (FP) • Craig Blais

Mrs. Dumpty (FP) • Chana Bloch

The Declarable Future (4L) • Jennifer Boyden

The Mouths of Grazing Things (B) • Jennifer Boyden

Help Is on the Way (4L) • John Brehm

Sea of Faith (B) • John Brehm

Reunion (FP) • Fleda Brown

Brief Landing on the Earth's Surface (B) • Juanita Brunk

Ejo: Poems, Rwanda, 1991–1994 (FP) • Derick Burleson

Jagged with Love (B) • Susanna Childress

Almost Nothing to Be Scared Of (4L) • David Clewell

The Low End of Higher Things • David Clewell

Now We're Getting Somewhere (FP) • David Clewell

Taken Somehow by Surprise (4L) • David Clewell

Borrowed Dress (FP) • Cathy Colman

Places/Everyone (B) • Jim Daniels

Show and Tell • Jim Daniels

Darkroom (B) • Jazzy Danziger

And Her Soul Out of Nothing (B) • Olena Kalytiak Davis

My Favorite Tyrants (B) • Joanne Diaz

Talking to Strangers (B) • Patricia Dobler

The Golden Coin (4L) • Alan Feldman

Immortality (4L) • Alan Feldman

(B) = Winner of the Brittingham Prize in Poetry
(FP) = Winner of the Felix Pollak Prize in Poetry
(4L) = Winner of the Four Lakes Prize in Poetry

A Sail to Great Island (FP) • Alan Feldman

The Word We Used for It (B) • Max Garland

A Field Guide to the Heavens (B) • Frank X. Gaspar

The Royal Baker's Daughter (FP) • Barbara Goldberg

Funny (FP) • Jennifer Michael Hecht

The Legend of Light (FP) • Bob Hicok

Sweet Ruin (B) • Tony Hoagland

Partially Excited States (FP) • Charles Hood

Ripe (FP) • Roy Jacobstein

Saving the Young Men of Vienna (B) • David Kirby

Falling Brick Kills Local Man (FP) • Mark Kraushaar

Last Seen (FP) • Jacqueline Jones LaMon

The Lightning That Strikes the Neighbors' House (FP) • Nick Lantz

You, Beast (B) • Nick Lantz

The Explosive Expert's Wife • Shara Lessley

The Unbeliever (B) • Lisa Lewis

Slow Joy (B) • Stephanie Marlis

Acts of Contortion (B) • Anna George Meek

Bardo (B) • Suzanne Paola

Meditations on Rising and Falling (B) • Philip Pardi

Old and New Testaments (B) • Lynn Powell

Season of the Second Thought (FP) • Lynn Powell

A Path between Houses (B) • Greg Rappleye

The Book of Hulga (FP) • Rita Mae Reese

Don't Explain (FP) • Betsy Sholl

Late Psalm • Betsy Sholl

Otherwise Unseeable (4L) • Betsy Sholl

Blood Work (FP) • Matthew Siegel

The Year We Studied Women (FP) • Bruce Snider

Bird Skin Coat (B) • Angela Sorby

The Sleeve Waves (FP) • Angela Sorby

Wait (B) • Alison Stine

Hive (B) • Christina Stoddard

The Red Virgin: A Poem of Simone Weil (B) • Stephanie Strickland

The Room Where I Was Born (B) • Brian Teare

Fragments in Us: Recent and Earlier Poems (FP) • Dennis Trudell

The Apollonia Poems (4L) • Judith Vollmer

Level Green (B) • Judith Vollmer

Reactor • Judith Vollmer

Voodoo Inverso (FP) • Mark Wagenaar

Hot Popsicles • Charles Harper Webb

Liver (FP) • Charles Harper Webb

The Blue Hour (B) • Jennifer Whitaker

Centaur (B) • Greg Wrenn

Pocket Sundial (B) • Lisa Zeidner